Mystical Mandala
COLORING BOOK

ALBERTA HUTCHINSON

DOVER PUBLICATIONS, INC.
MINEOLA, NEW YORK

NOTE

The mandala, a name derived from the Sanskrit word for "circle," is a Hindu and Buddhist symbol that represents the universe and its energy. These symmetrical geometric designs are traditionally used for meditative purposes by drawing your eye to the center of the circle. The intricate patterns making up these exotic mandalas hold a special significance and provide a focal point for meditation.

This striking collection includes an assortment of thirty plates that will delight and challenge artists of all ages. Use your own creativity to color these mystical motifs that symbolize the universe, wholeness, and eternity.

Copyright

Copyright © 2007 by Alberta Hutchinson
All rights reserved.

Bibliographical Note

Mystical Mandala Coloring Book is a new work, first published by Dover Publications, Inc., in 2007.

International Standard Book Number

ISBN-13: 978-0-486-45694-2
ISBN-10: 0-486-45694-3

Manufactured in the United States by RR Donnelley
45694323   2015
www.doverpublications.com

1

4

14

22